Amazing Animals
Elephants

Jacqueline Dineen

WEIGL PUBLISHERS INC.

Published by Weigl Publishers Inc.
350 5th Avenue, Suite 3304, PMB 6G
New York, NY 10118-0069

Amazing Animals series ©2010
WEIGL PUBLISHERS INC. www.weigl.com
Library of Congress Cataloging-in-
Publication Data

Library of Congress Cataloging-in-
Publication Data available upon request.
Fax 1-866-44-WEIGL for the attention of
the Publishing Records department.

ISBN 978-1-60596-154-5 (hard cover)
ISBN 978-1-60596-155-2 (soft cover)

Editor
Heather Kissock
Design and Layout
Terry Paulhus, Kathryn Livingstone

Photograph Credits
Every reasonable effort has been
made to trace ownership and to obtain
permission to reprint copyright material.
The publishers would be pleased to have
any errors or omissions brought to their
attention so that they may be corrected
in subsequent printings.

Weigl acknowledges Getty Images as its
primary image supplier for this title.

Printed in China
1 2 3 4 5 6 7 8 9 0 13 12 11 10 09

About This Book

This book tells you all about
elephants. Find out where they
live and what they eat. Discover
how you can help to protect them.
You can also read about them in
myths and legends from around
the world.

Words in **bold** are explained in the
Words to Know section at the back
of the book.

Useful Websites

Addresses in this book
take you to the home
pages of websites that
have information
about elephants.

All of the Internet URLs given in
the book were valid at the time
of publication. However, due to
the dynamic nature of the Internet,
some addresses may have changed,
or sites may have ceased to exist
since publication. While the author
and publisher regret any
inconvenience this may cause
readers, no responsibility for any
such changes can be accepted by
either the author or the publisher.

Contents

Meet the Elephant

The elephant is the largest animal that lives on land. It has a huge, bulky body and a long nose called a trunk. Two curved tusks grow on either side of the trunk. Tusks are long, sharp teeth. They are made of a hard material called **ivory**.

▼ A very special feature of the elephant is its long trunk.

There are two types of elephants, African elephants and Asian elephants.

Useful Websites

www.indianapoliszoo.com

Learn about the elephants living at the Indianapolis Zoo at this website.

Elephant Facts

- The tallest known elephant was more than 13 feet (4 meters) high. Its leg was taller than a human.

- Elephants are very large and heavy, but they can run faster than people.

▲ The elephant's wrinkly skin keeps the animal cool by trapping moisture in the folds.

A Very Unusual Animal

An elephant's trunk gives it a strange appearance. The trunk is the elephant's nose, which it uses to breathe. An elephant also uses its trunk like an arm to pick things up and to put food into its mouth.

At the end of an elephant's trunk are clasping parts known as "fingers." The elephant uses these to grasp small objects such as leaves.

▲ An Asian elephant has smaller ears than an African elephant.

African or Asian?

- An African elephant has very large ears. An Asian elephant's ears are smaller.

- An African elephant has two "fingers" at the end of its trunk. Asian elephants have one.

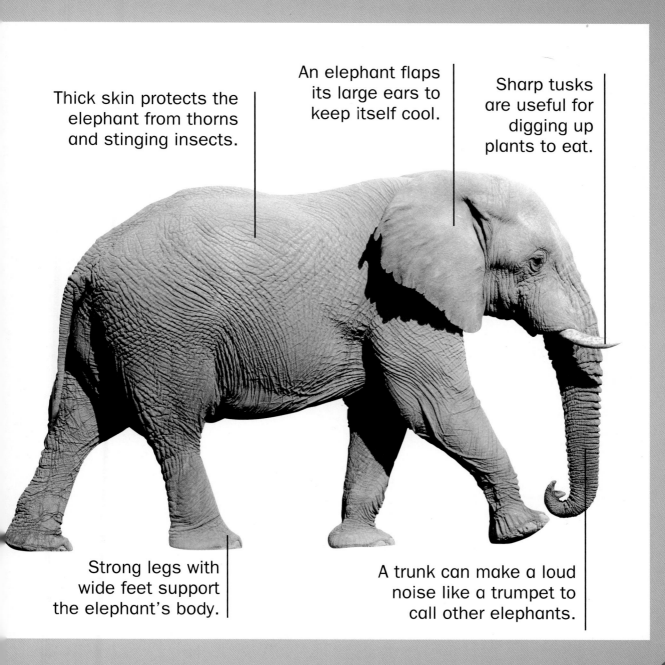

Thick skin protects the elephant from thorns and stinging insects.

An elephant flaps its large ears to keep itself cool.

Sharp tusks are useful for digging up plants to eat.

Strong legs with wide feet support the elephant's body.

A trunk can make a loud noise like a trumpet to call other elephants.

Where Do They Live?

There are many more African elephants than Asian elephants. African elephants live in most parts of Africa. They like places that have grass and trees to eat, such as the African **savanna**.

▼ In India, some Asian elephants carry people and goods.

Many Asian elephants live in forests. Asian elephants are found in India, Indonesia, Thailand, and other neighboring countries.

Useful Websites

www.elephants.com

Visit this website to learn about a U.S. refuge for Asian elephants.

Elephant Range

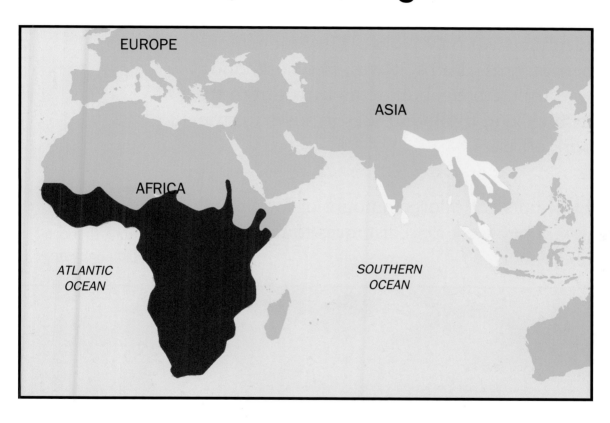

EUROPE

ASIA

AFRICA

ATLANTIC
OCEAN

SOUTHERN
OCEAN

N
W · E
S

0 500 1,000 km
0 311 622 mi

■ African Elephants
□ Asian Elephants

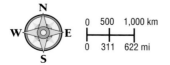

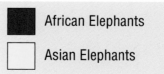

What Do They Eat?

Elephants eat only plants. They munch on berries, grass, herbs, leaves, tree bark, and wild fruit. An elephant tears leaves from trees with its long trunk and uses its tusks to strip bark off trees.

Elephants eat a large amount of food each day. They walk long distances to find food and water.

▼ An elephant can stretch its trunk to reach high branches.

What a Thirst!

An elephant can drink 35 gallons (159 L) of water in just one day. That is like drinking 1,120 cans of soda.

▲ To drink, an elephant sucks up water with its trunk. Then, it sprays the water into its mouth.

Family Life

Female elephants and their babies live in close family groups. The leader of the group is the **matriarch**. This is the oldest mother elephant. Adult male elephants, or **bulls**, do not live in family groups.

There are up to 25 elephants in a family. When the young female elephants grow up, they stay with the family. If the family grows too big, some of the elephants form a new group.

▶ Adult elephants protect younger ones from danger.

Leaving Home

Young male elephants leave the family group when they are 10 to 15 years old. They live alone, or with one or two other males.

▲ When a family of elephants come across water, it will stop for a drink.

Growing Up

A mother elephant gives birth to one baby, called a **calf**. At first, the baby elephant cannot walk very far or use its trunk. It stays very close to its mother and drinks milk from her body.

After about six months, a calf learns how to use its trunk. It begins to eat plants and drink water. Young calves often play together.

▶ A young elephant stays close to its mother until it is about four years old.

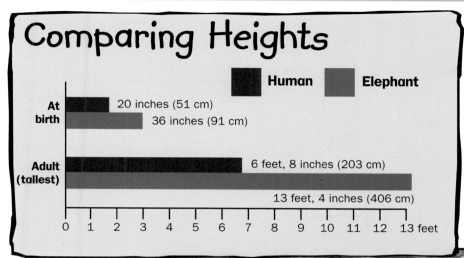

Comparing Heights

■ Human　**■ Elephant**

At birth
20 inches (51 cm)
36 inches (91 cm)

Adult (tallest)
6 feet, 8 inches (203 cm)
13 feet, 4 inches (406 cm)

0　1　2　3　4　5　6　7　8　9　10　11　12　13 feet

▲ A baby elephant continues drinking its mother's milk until it is about three years old.

Friends and Enemies

Adult elephants are safe from most **predators** because they are so big. Elephants are not meat-eaters, so they do not attack other animals.

▼ A fierce lion will not fight with an adult elephant.

Lions and crocodiles will kill baby elephants for food. If enemies are nearby, the mother elephants will stand in a ring around their babies to protect them.

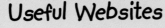

Useful Websites

www.elephanttrust.org

This website has photographs of elephants.

Getting Along

Elephants are usually friendly to other elephants. Sometimes, large male elephants wrestle with each other to find out who is stronger.

▲ Elephants share their home with other animals.

Under Threat

People are elephants' worst enemies. Many elephants are killed for their ivory tusks. In the past, ivory was very valuable, but today, selling ivory is against the law. Today, fewer elephants are killed for their tusks.

▼ In many places, it is against the law to sell jewelry and ornaments made from elephants' tusks.

Elephants are losing their **habitats**. People have chopped down trees and built towns in places where elephants once lived.

Useful Websites
www.kidsplanet.org/
factsheets/elephant.html
Read about African elephants and
their features at this site.

▲ An elephant has no chance against a human with a gun.

Helping Elephants

There are many parks in Africa where elephants can live in safety. Special groups of people look after young elephants whose families have been killed.

Myths and Legends

People have always viewed elephants as gentle giants. Many people in Africa think that elephants bring good luck and happiness. When elephants trample crops, some people blame an evil spirit instead of the elephants.

▼ In India, elephants are sometimes used in festivals.

Elephant Gods

People in India and other parts of Asia worship gods that have elephant heads. For those who follow the Hindu religion, Ganesha is the elephant god of wisdom and good luck.

▼ The Hindu god Ganesha has an elephant's head.

Good Fortune

In some parts of the world, people put small statues of elephants in doorways. They believe that the statues keep their houses safe from evil spirits.

Quiz

1. How does an elephant keep cool?
(a) **by wiggling its trunk** (b) **by flapping its ears**
(c) **by waving its tail**

2. Which animals may attack baby elephants?
(a) **zebras** (b) **giraffes** (c) **lions**

3. What do elephants eat?
(a) **plants** (b) **meat** (c) **fish**

4. What is a tusk?
(a) **a long tooth** (b) **a long claw**
(c) **a long nose**

5. At what age do young elephants start to eat plants?
(a) **six days** (b) **six weeks** (c) **six months**

Find out More

To find out more about elephants, visit the websites in this book. You can also write to these organizations.

African Wildlife Foundation
1717 Massachusetts Avenue NW
Washington, DC 20036

International Wildlife Coalition
70 East Falmouth Hwy
East Falmouth, MA 02536-5957

Words to Know

bulls
male elephants

calf
a young elephant

habitats
places where an animal usually lives

ivory
a hard, white material that elephants' tusks are made of

matriarch
the oldest mother elephant in a family; she is the leader of the family

predators
animals that hunt other animals for food

savanna
the grasslands of Africa

Index